Booklet Belongs To:

____

Trace and color the Easter bunny.

Color the Easter egg.

Help the Easter bunny find his egg.

Connect the dots to make an Easter egg.

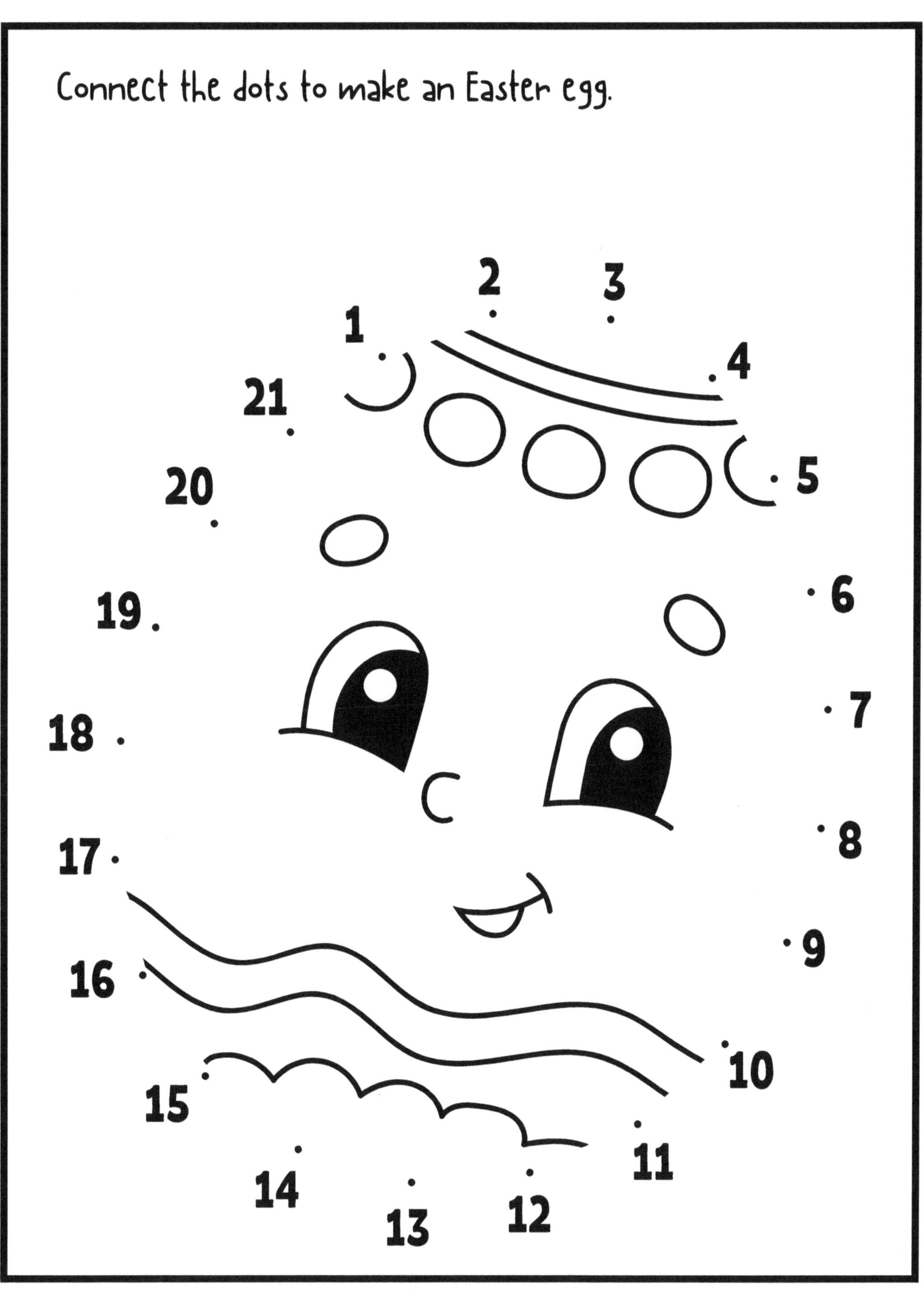

Trace and color the Easter chick.

Color the Easter bunny.

Help the Easter bunny find his egg:

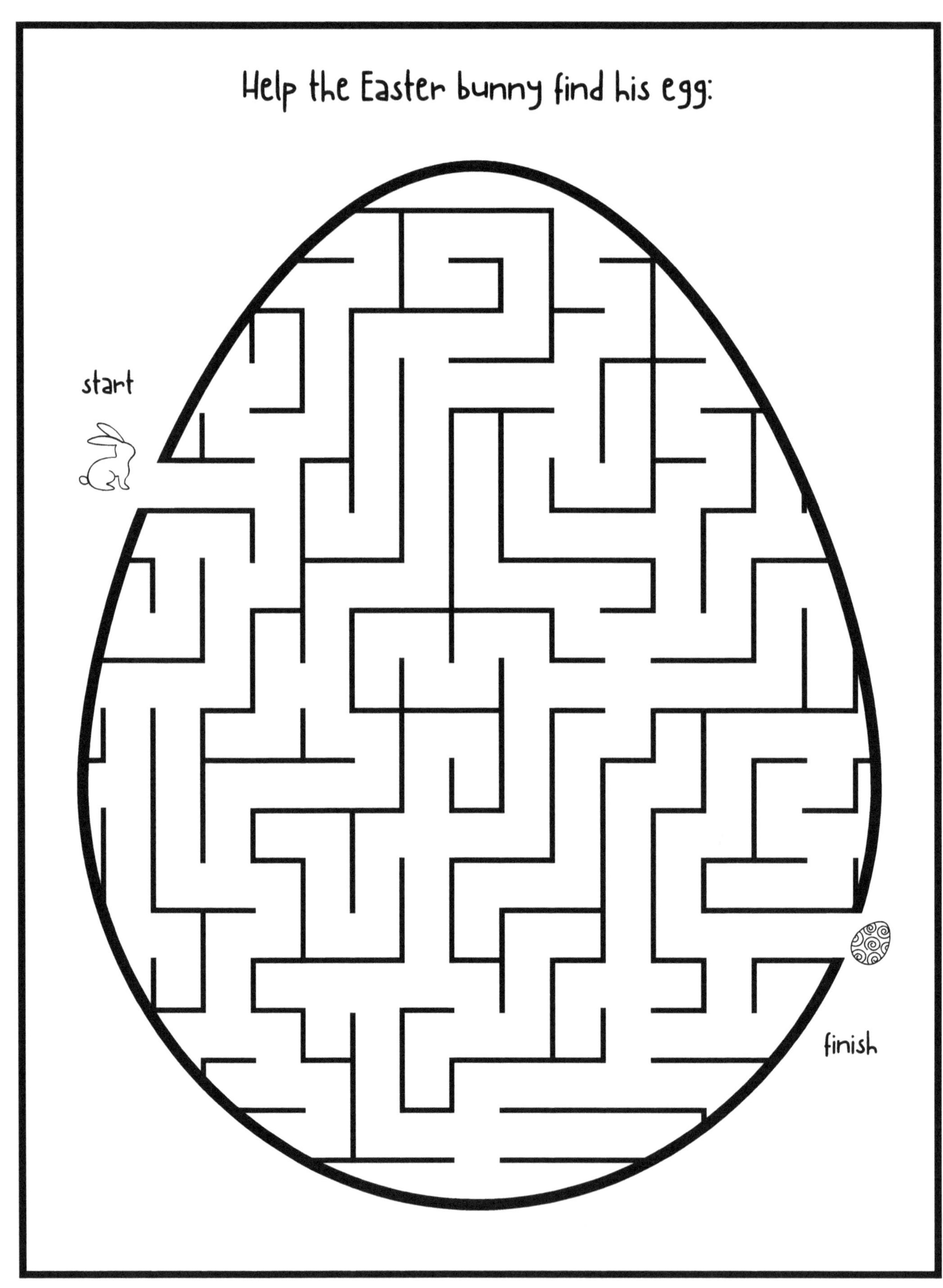

Connect the dots to make an Easter tree.

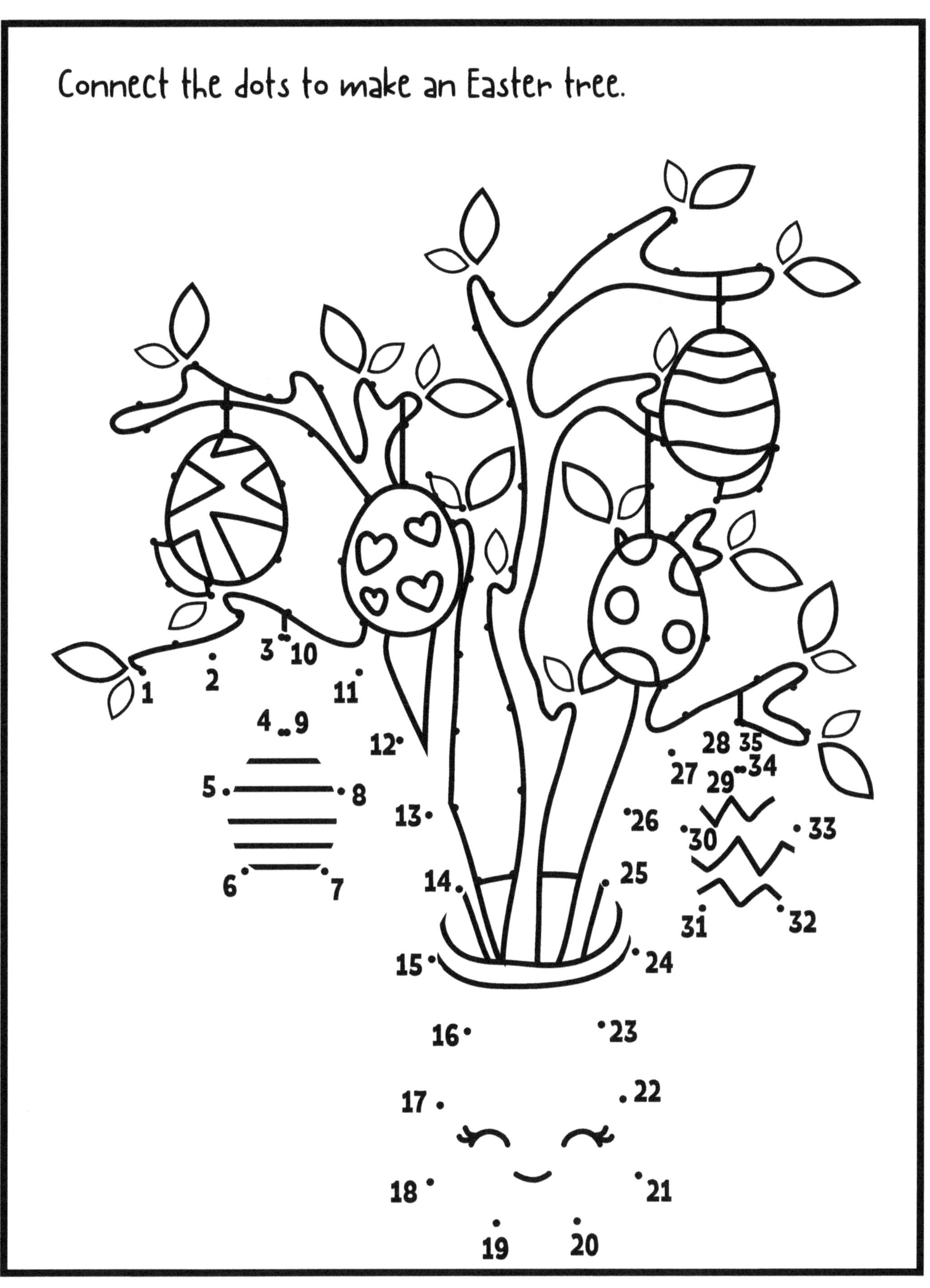

Trace and color the Easter basket.

Help the Easter bunny find his egg.

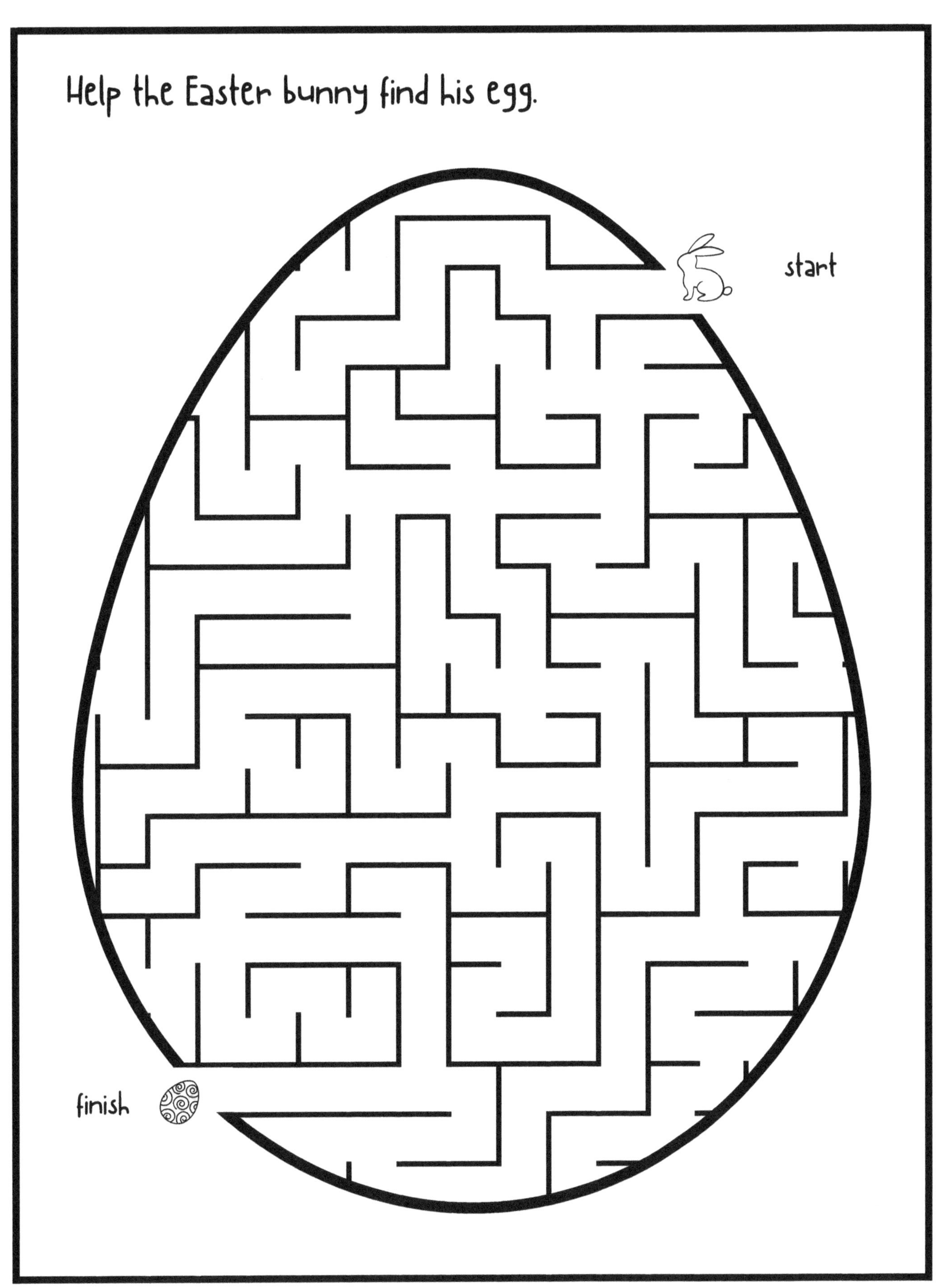

Connect the dots to make an Easter basket.

Trace and color the Easter egg.

Help the Easter bunny find his egg.

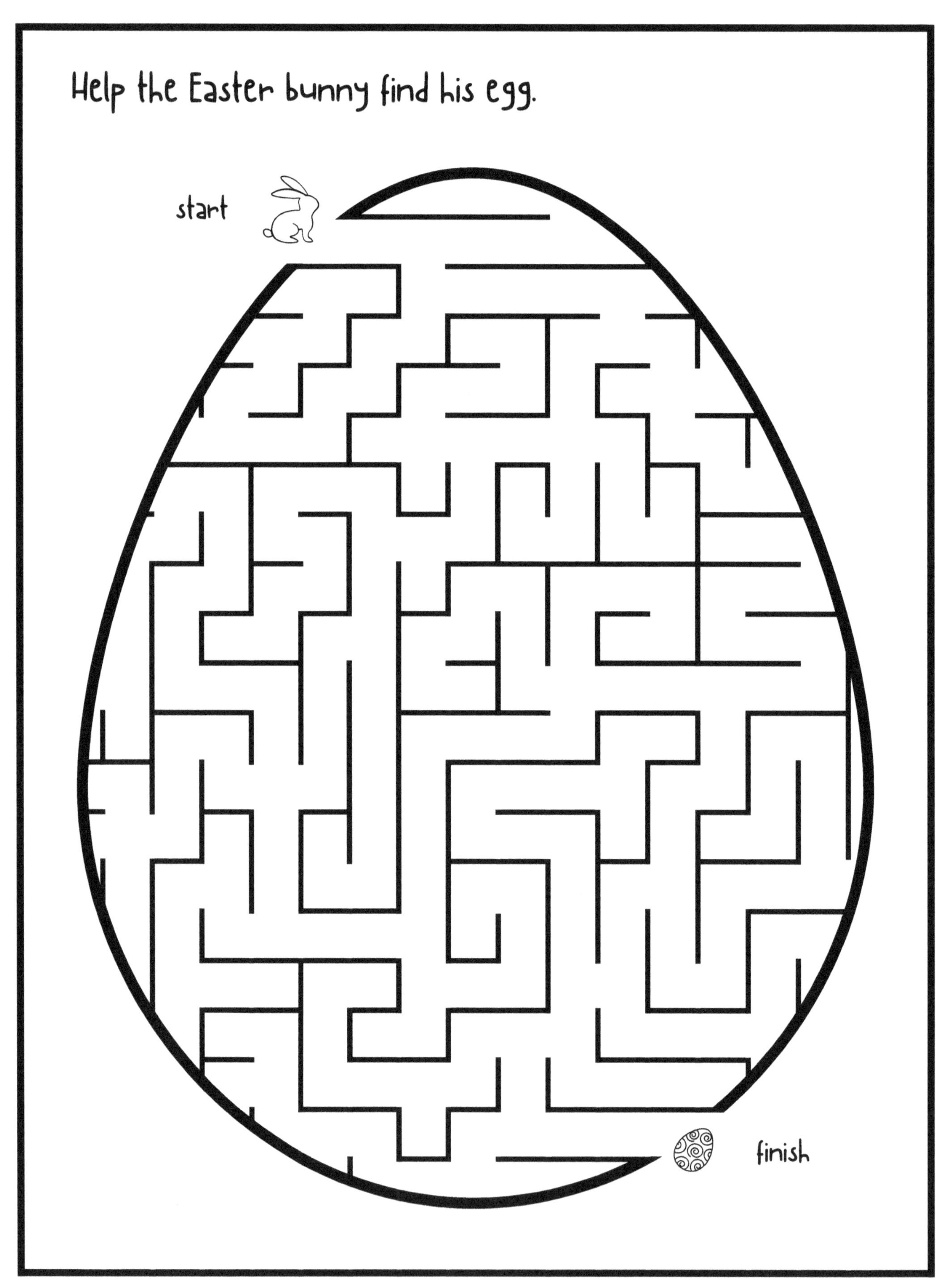

Connect the dots to make a chicken.

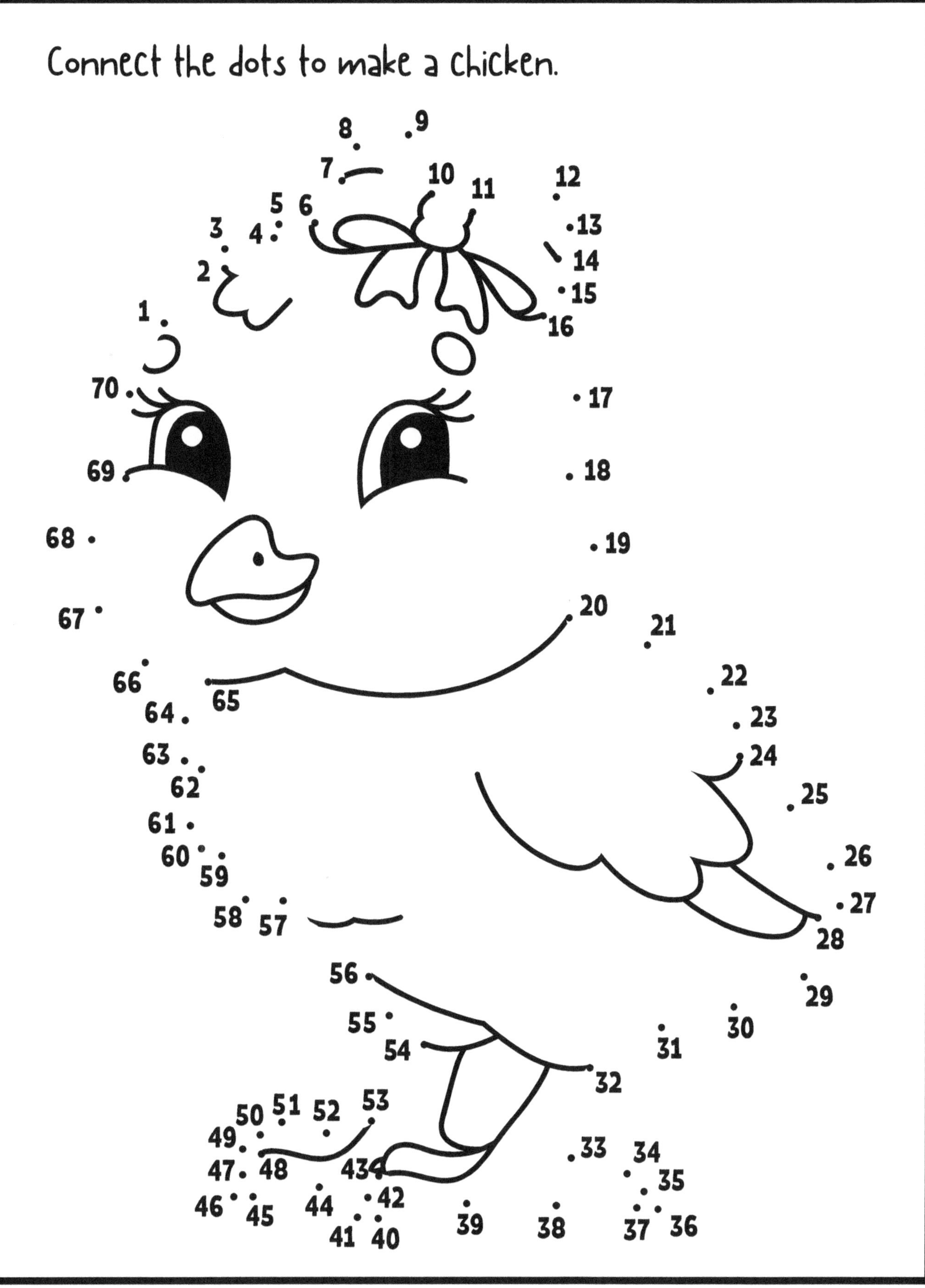

Color the Easter bunny.

Trace and color the Easter tree.

Trace and colori the Easter basket.

Color the Easter bunny.

Trace and color the Easter vase.

EASTER
Word Search Puzzle

```
B A S K E T D A S F C
U Z I Y V X S J D C H
N P D B N H U N T A O
N C A N D Y N J T R C
Y Q E G G S D G I R O
G R A S S J A R B O L
O A S X O O Y E B T A
M B T C H I C K A Z T
K B E F L O W E R S E
E A R S A P R I L L A
```

BASKET	CARROT	RABBIT
BUNNY	EGGS	FLOWERS
EARS	APRIL	CHOCOLATE
EASTER	CHICK	SUNDAY
GRASS	HUNT	CANDY

Dear Easter Bunny
Love from

POSTCARD

POSTCARD

THE END